The Great Escape:
Background and Memoirs
of the Liberian Civil War

The Great Escape: Background and Memoirs of the Liberian Civil War

Dorothy D. Johnson

iUniverse, Inc.

New York Lincoln Shanghai

The Great Escape: Background and Memoirs of the Liberian Civil War

iUniverse books may be ordered through booksellers or by contacting:

iUniverse
2021 Pine Lake Road, Suite 100
Lincoln, NE 68512
www.iuniverse.com
1-800-Authors (1-800-288-4677)

Because of the dynamic nature of the Internet, any Web addresses or links contained in this book may have changed since publication and may no longer be valid.

The views expressed in this work are solely those of the author and do not necessarily reflect the views of the publisher, and the publisher hereby disclaims any responsibility for them.

ISBN: 978-0-595-47288-8 (pbk)
ISBN: 978-0-595-91565-1 (ebk)

Printed in the United States of America

This book is dedicated to the glory of God.

"For we brought nothing into this world, and it is certain we can carry nothing out."

—1 TIMOTHY 6:7

Contents

Foreword

Liberia. The name itself invokes images of happy natives dancing, ecstatic to be free. As recounted in the brief history at the beginning of this memoir, Liberia was founded by ex-slaves from America. What could be more heartwarming than a story about natives plucked from Africa, shackled into slave ships and dragged to the New World but whose descendants were freed, reversing those steps to sail back to their homeland and start a new country? Freedom, liberty, boats landing on the shore to settle an independent country. The very heart of American values, these are. The capital, Monrovia, is even named after President Monroe.

But dig a little deeper and the story is much more complicated. The American 'benevolent' societies that assisted the former slaves to return to Africa did so in order to remove the freed men and women from the communities where they lived so they wouldn't give ideas to those slaves who were not yet free. So the assistance was not based on humanitarian or ethical grounds, but much more from a practical, self-serving motive. And those first Liberians were not uniformly kind and accepting of all who might want to be part of the new country. Many enslaved the local inhabitants, with heavy taxation and forced labor.

But the Liberia I saw when I first arrived (on a plane, not a boat) in 1985 was intriguing. The saggy-roofed old houses that looked as if they should be in Mississippi, not Africa. The plump ladies decked out in dark suits and broad-rimmed hats with nets on their way to church on Sunday morning. And the red and white-striped flag with white stars on a blue square that made me think all the government buildings were part of the US Embassy until I noticed the slight differences between the Liberian and American flags.

And then there was Dorothy. She was the manager of the survey project that I was helping the Ministry of Planning and Economic Affairs to implement. It involved selecting a sample of households scattered in 150 communities throughout the country, mapping and listing those areas, developing the questionnaire, training the interviewers and, worst of all, arranging for 7 or 8 sturdy 4-wheel drive vehicles that we could use for about 4 months. There were myriads of details to deal with and Dorothy did, without losing her cool. She was a serious person and my colleagues and I used to remark how nice it was when we managed to get Dorothy to smile. It was a warm, engaging smile, despite its rarity.

Though we worked together on many of my visits to plan and assist with the survey, and I met her ever-helpful husband and her three young boys, it was not until she came to the U.S. to work on the final report of the survey that I really bonded with Dorothy. She visited my home several times and though she is younger than I, it was her quiet dignity and maturity that I noticed and respected. We talked of relationships and she had wise words. Like a sister would.

After that visit, we rarely stayed in touch. She wrote that she left the government to take a job with the UN. But I didn't know much about her life. And then the conflict came and I worried about her and all the other Liberians I had met. The radio was filled with horror stories and one Liberian who was in the US said he hadn't heard from his wife or children in months and had no idea if they were still alive.

And then finally, I heard from Dorothy. A letter saying she was in Nigeria. From then on, we stayed in touch, writing and sometimes calling. Until she came to the US and she and I tried to get her husband and children here as well. When she told me the story of their final months in Monrovia, I told her she should write a book. And that is what she did. Happy reading!

Anne Cross
Maryland, USA

Author's Note

A significant part of this book is based on my memoirs as I remembered and wrote them during the Liberian Civil War.

In some instances, I have used the actual names of people in the narrative. In other parts, the names have been changed to protect certain individuals' privacy.

Thanks and Appreciation

I thank Almighty God for giving me the strength and courage to finally publish my memoirs after years of procrastination.

My profound thanks and appreciation go to my family: my husband Ben Sr., our sons: Marvin, Ben Jr., and Arnold for standing by me through thick and thin as we lived the ordeal together.

I also thank my parents, Mr. and Mrs. David D. Chieh Sr. for their relentless prayers and support during the war and after our escape.

My heartfelt thanks go to my siblings: David Chieh Jr., Patrick, Antoinette, Christopher, Nehemiah and Emmanuel (late) for their love and support.

Special thanks and appreciation go to Ms. Anne R. Cross for her encouragement and continuous support even after the war. She is a very special lady!
Many people have rendered assistance to me one way or the other in getting my family over to the U.S. Among them are my brother David Chieh Jr. and his family, Rev. Sue Job, Representative Kate Auspitz, Rev. Amy Alletzhauser and my church family at the Centralville United Methodist Church in Lowell, Massachusetts and many more.

I appreciate the critique and suggestions made by my friend and colleague respectively, Ms. Mary Keough of Lowell and Mr. Eric Moore of the St. Ann's School, Methuen. I thank you all so much.

Lastly, but by no means the least, I am very grateful and thankful for the timely intervention of the Ghanaian government through the former president, General Jerry Rawlings who sent the cargo ship to evacuate hundreds of thousands of stranded people in Liberia. Without this noble humanitarian gesture, my family and I may have been counted among the dead.

I am also very thankful and grateful to President George W. Bush and the American people. President Bush's intercession to remove the warlord, Charles Taylor brought an end to the seemingly incessant war that ravaged the small country and its people for over a decade.

Introduction

As I sit back and reminisce into the past, at best, I can envision my life in groups of decades such as the 1950's, 60's, 70's, 80's, 90's and so on.

My life began on November 10, 1953 in a hospital in a West African nation I did not select by choice, but happened to be born there by my Togolese mother Comfort Clement Chieh. My father David Chieh Sr. originated from Grancess, Grand Kru County, Liberia.

Most of my life has been a mixture of good times and difficult times. I have never been proud of the fact that I was born in another African country other than my own Liberia. But as a firm believer in truth, this revealed fact haunted me most of the time, especially growing up in the Liberian Society, where African foreigners were often stereotyped. Liberians paid dearly for this negative attitude, as tens of thousands of us became refugees in neighboring African countries. Future generations of Liberians were born in these nations of Ghana, Nigeria, Sierra-Leone, Ivory Coast and Togo.

My siblings and I were raised with loving care, yet with very strict discipline. Not surprising that my paternal grandfather was a policeman. My grandmother died when my dad was a very young child. I enjoyed the nurture of my maternal grandparents for a very long time.

Years later, five other brothers and a sister were added to the family making me the eldest of several children.

My years in primary school were okay. I used to walk several miles to and from school. During my primary school days, I used to be the envy of the entire school, year after year. I usually carried a letter of excuse to the headmistress for permission to wear my hair long—that we don't wear our hair short in my country. This was a real source of envy in an all girl convent school where every other girl had a short hair-cut resembling that of a boy. Even the teachers did not have hair as long as mine.

The decade of the 60's brought a rather dramatic turn in my life. I was about 12–13 years old when my family decided to leave the foreign land and resettle back home in Liberia. I suffered a bit of a cultural shock because things were done so liberally in Liberia, as compared to the very strict British way we were brought up. My classmates in junior high school went to school with hair pressed and styled, finger nails painted and so on and so forth, it was quite surprising to me. I just used to wear my naturally long hair clean and plaited and dressed neatly and simply.

At home in Liberia, once again, I attended an all girls' convent school called St. Teresa's Convent. When I was promoted to the ninth grade, my Algebra teacher, Mr. Eustace made a positive change in my life. He made algebra as simple as 'abc' and brought out my love for math as my favorite subject. I used to do very well in math from the ninth grade and all through high school.

I also remembered Mr. Eliott. He was my twelfth grade math teacher. Whenever he gives quiz or test, he would arrange the papers from lowest scores to the highest. My paper was always the last to be given, being the highest score. He would shower me with all sorts of praises, giving me titles like "your majesty, your honor" etc. I usually blushed but enjoyed all the pampering.

The decade of the 70's took me through college where I studied Sociology and Demography. I met the man who would become my husband, during my first year in college. I also met the Lord and became a born-again Christian. While in college, I was a staunch member of the Varsity Christian Fellowship. I enjoyed fellowship with other believers, attended camp meetings and so on. I remembered that it was during that period that the world renowned Evangelist, Billy Graham visited the University of Liberia's campus where he conducted a crusade. It was a huge success.

When I graduated from college, I was given a job at the Ministry of Planning and Economic Affairs because of the brilliant paper I presented at the Monrovia City Hall. It was on the analysis of the 1962-1974 Censuses of Liberia. The late Mr. Samuel Greene, an Assistant Minister of Planning and Statistics, was so impressed with my presentation that he offered me a position at the Ministry.

I worked in the Population Division of the Ministry as Research officer for a couple of years. I got married on May 5, 1979 to my college sweet heart and we started life together.

In 1980, we had our first of three sons. It was also a very difficult and decisive time, because I was awarded a scholarship on my job to do graduate studies in population statistics. I had to leave my family back home including our first son who was just about six months old.

By August 1980, I enrolled at the Georgetown University in Washington D.C. as well as the International Statistical Program Center in Maryland. I couldn't bear to be alone without my family. Soon afterwards, my husband and son joined me in the United States of America. After two years of dedicated hard work, I obtained an M.A. degree in demography and headed home to contribute my quota to the development process of my country.

I continued to work in the population division of the Ministry of Planning and Economic Affairs as senior research officer until an opportunity became available for me to work with the United Nations Fund for Population Activities (UNFPA). In 1988, I became National Program Officer for UNFPA, a position, I held dearly until the civil war.

As a family, my husband and I had just built our five bedroom house located in Brewerville in the outskirt of Monrovia. We had finally settled down to enjoy the fruits of our labor and hard work that we endured all throughout our lives.

Disappointingly, every thing changed for the worse. It was like waking up from a nightmare; everything became dark, gloomy and scary! All our hopes and aspiration for a better life were dashed and shattered like an expensive piece of china ware.

Bam! The Liberian Civil War began! Our lives became transformed and trans-fixed. Everyday became a struggle laden with fear of the unknown. We had never experienced war before!

We don't even know what to expect, maybe we will live or die!

The story of rebel incursion or worse still, an invasion, may have sounded quite extraneous, remote or even a fable to the small, approximately 2.3 million peace-loving Liberians anytime before the fateful month of December, 1989. Like a horror story, it became a reality!

Section One :
Background/History

At this juncture, the following sections reveal in chronological order the developments of events that culminated into the Liberian Civil War.

Its history throws light on several decades of political and developmental digress.

According to Levy 1998, very little is known about the people who inhabited the land that became Liberia in the early 19th century. The country is Africa's oldest republic and dates back to 1822, when United States philanthropic organizations succeeded in establishing an African home for former slaves.

In 1816, the United States began negotiations with local rulers over the possibility of acquiring sufficient land to form a settlement for freed slaves.

The following year the American Colonization Society was founded with the intension of resettling emancipated slaves and freeborn Africans, and by 1821, the society was able to purchase the area around Cape Mesurado, later renaming the settlement Monrovia. Within a year, the first people arrived from the United States, and in 1824, the name Liberia was adopted, (Levy, 1998).

The small nation of Liberia covers a land area of 38,250 sq. miles. Geographically, it is bounded in the north by the Republic of Guinea, in the west, by Sierra Leone, in the east, by the Republic of Cote d' Ivoire and in the south by the Atlantic Ocean, (Liberian Demographic and Health Survey,1988).

In terms of population size, Liberia is also relatively small. In 1989, the estimated population was 2.3 million people. A significant proportion of the population is rural: sixty percent, while forty percent lived in urban areas. The dominant urban center, Monrovia, which is also the capital of the country, was a bustling cosmopolitan city with a population size of nearly half a million people.

Since its inception as an independent nation on July 26, 1847, about nineteen presidents have had turns to rule the small West African nation.

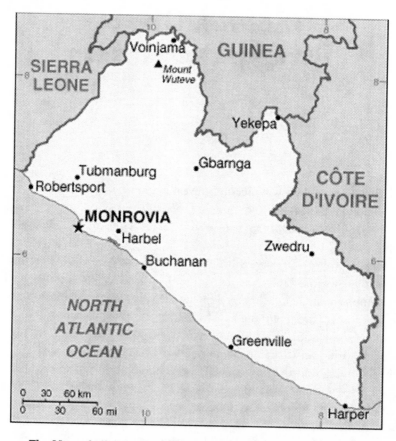

The Map of Liberia showing the capital Monrovia and some major cities.

The Truncated Problem

In the strict sense of the word, Liberia being an independent nation was never 'colonized' by any of the super powers such as the United States of America, Great Britain, France, Germany etc. Its long traditional affiliation with America was promulgated when the emancipated slaves who sailed back to Africa from America, made their abode in Liberia, in search of a new homeland.

Its foundation in 1822 as a home for emancipated black slaves from the United States bears noble testimony to its name and its motto: "The love of liberty brought us here."(Levy, 1998).

The free slaves known as 'Americo Liberians', didn't have an easy settlement. They were met with hostility and feuding by the indigenes of the land. After several years of hostility, the Americo-Liberians managed to subdue the natives and thereby began their oligarchy which lasted for over a century.

On the one hand, many positive contributions can be attributed to the Americo-Liberians: the spread of Christianity, establishment of schools, churches and hospitals as they exhibited skills they acquired from their former masters.

Liberia's seventeenth president, William V.S. Tubman was an Americo-Liberian who placed Liberia on the international arena of fame when he established the 'Open Door Policy'. Through this policy, Liberia became a gateway for foreign investors, business men, traders etc. They invested and traded freely in the country and were guaranteed freedom to remit earnings without excessive restriction. The Policy which was intended to enhance the economic viability of the country, which depended on rubber and iron ore as its export commodities, retrogressively placed the entire economy in the complete monopoly of foreign businessmen, most of whom were Lebanese, Indians, and other Europeans.

Under the open door policy, these foreign merchants established various retail and wholesale businesses in Liberia. They encountered very little competition from Liberian businessmen.

On the other hand, although the oligarchy of the Americo-Liberians brought some positive changes, its negative consequences were quite significant. The earliest constitution was patterned after the United States; however, it denied the majority of the populace their constitutional rights. The indigenous tribes were not treated as equals; political elite developed out of the early America-Liberians and their descendants (Levi, 1998).

The pace of development was very slow; education and infra-structural development were not widespread. After a hundred years of independence, recent estimates showed a literacy rate less than thirty percent. Agricultural productivity was at its lowest ebb, foreign investors used most of the land to cultivate rubber and mine iron ore. A great state of dependency was created as the populace relied greatly on imported goods, even the staple food, rice, was mostly imported.

From the social perspective, there was no real integration between the Americo-Liberians and the indigenous Liberians. There was an imaginary line of separatism or segregation existing between the two groups. The Americo-Liberians were looked at as the privileged class while the indigenous masses were stereotyped as the 'country people'. Intermarriages were rare.

During the reign of the eighteenth president, William R. Tolbert, also a descendant of the America-Liberian elites, there was an effort to narrow the differences between the two groups. Nation-wide suffrage was introduced and the Liberian constitution was amended to disallow any president to go for reelection. Scholarships were awarded to qualified indigenes for higher education, a few intermarriages began to occur, and some good jobs were given to indigenes, although not in strategic areas of the economy or political structure. Most of these privileged indigenes were very educated or were raised by Americo-Liberian families. Some of these indigenes were made to drop their native names and adopt the names of their guardians.

These turned out to be too little too late.

Worst still, in the mid-1970s there was a dramatic drop in the price of iron ore and rubber in the world market. Many Liberians lost their jobs as businesses were forced to cut back. There was a sharp decline in the economy, which Liberians blamed on President Tolbert, (Stewart, 1992).

The economy continued to take a downward plunge as the price of rice rose in 1979. According to Stewart, 1992, many Liberians could no longer afford to feed their families and became furious. Widespread demonstrations and rioting took place in Monrovia and other cities in Liberia.

Many put the blame squarely on the shoulders of Presidents Tubman and Tolbert. The indigenous people felt that they had been ignored for too long.

Despite all the attempts made by Tubman and Tolbert, Liberia's money and power lay with the Settlers or Americo-Liberians, (Stewart, 1992).

The 1980 Coup D'Etat

The hostility that caused the riots and the demonstrations had a far more serious consequence. According to Stewart, 1992, a political group opposed to president Tolbert, called the People's Progressive Party (PPP), was formed. In March 1980, demonstrations organized by the PPP were held throughout Liberia. During the course of the protests, more than 135 indigenous demonstrators were shot by the Liberian soldiers.

As a direct result, a military coup, or takeover of the government took place.

The dawn of April 12, 1980, marked the beginning of a new era in Liberia's history. It brought about the break in the oligarchy of the Americo-Liberians. On this day, President William R. Tolbert was brutally assassinated in a military coup-d-etat. A group of noncommissioned officers led by Thomas Quiwonkpa, Master Sergeant Doe and others seized power, and declared a junta called the "People's Redemption Council" or PRC. Samuel Doe was elected Chairman of the PRC and the first indigenous Head of State of Liberia.

The Coup relayed by the international press was recorded as one of the bloodiest in recent times. Ministers and officials of the late President Tolbert's regime, some of them with only the criterion of being Americo-Liberian were tied to wooden poles on the beach and gunned down like common criminals. The act which was widely condemned revealed years of deep hatred and strife between the indigenes and the Americo-Liberians.

Jubilant crowds were seen singing and dancing in the capital city of Monrovia and in many other towns in the Republic. People felt happy because they thought the start of Sgt. Doe's regime marked the end of long years of suppression, segregation and the birth of freedom from such social shackles. They thought the military takeover would bring about a new and fairer system of government.

From left to right, Sergeant Nicholas Podier, Sgt. Thomas Quiwonkpa, Master Sgt. Samuel Doe and Sgt. Weh Syen

The Man—Samuel K. Doe

Samuel K. Doe originated from a minority ethnic group called the Krahns. They are found in Grand Gedeh County in the southeastern part of Liberia. Samuel K. Doe, an offspring of illiterate parents was born on May 12, 1950. Based on empirical evidence, one can clearly deduce that this man had very little education as has been characteristic of most indigenes that joined the Liberian military.

Apart from being an indigene, the criteria for the selection of Doe as leader of the Coup d'etat remain a misery. It is perhaps best known to dissidents of the Tolbert regime and other international players who were responsible for his ascendancy into the highest office of the land.

The initial reign of Samuel K. Doe as commander-in-chief of Liberia was filled with pageantry among the people. He made sweeping and uncalculated changes such as doubling the salaries of army officers in an effort to pacify them. He also donated huge sums of money to various schools as well as built several market houses to win the support of people from the grass roots.

Two years after Doe came to power, his popularity began to dwindle. People began to feel the economic pinch because much of the country's resources were being squandered. Moreover, as the country's main export commodities, iron ore and rubber began to depreciate on the world market, there was a drop in Liberia's net revenue. Due to the fact that Liberia depends mainly on imported goods—both essential and luxury goods, government's expenditure became more than its generated revenue, plunging the country into a recession.

In a bid to safeguard the drooping economy and as advised by Doe's minister of economic affairs and planning, he began to institute drastic policies. The salaries of civil servants, was reduced twice, by 16 2/3 percent and 25 percent respectively. Saving bonds emerged but were never honored even when they reached maturity. Despite these drastic economic measures, the Doe government could not meet with the timely payment of civil servants' salaries. There was a back-log for up to three months of unpaid remuneration to civil servants.

The Emergence of a Dictator

As life began to get tougher and tougher for the average Liberian, rumors circulated that Doe was supposed to relinquish power to someone else or he should have served as a figure-head.

However, no sooner had Doe tasted the sweet buds of power and money, he began to emerge strong and mighty. He literarily became a 'Frankenstein' who no longer listened to his accomplices and some honest advisers.

The same ills that he initially accused the William R. Tolbert regime of having committed such as rampant corruption, nepotism, greed, selfishness, abuse of power, suppression, ethnicity, etc., became characteristics and traits of his government.

He started by exterminating members of his cohorts of twelve gallant men one after the other. Squander-mania was at its peak. Year after year, his officials and compatriots changed various models of cars; from the Volkswagen Brasilia to Honda and then to Mercedes Benz. Ethnicity and nepotism became the order of the day; mostly men of the Krahn tribe were placed in strategic areas of the political and economic structures. Any form of criticism was quickly repelled and the offender incarcerated or exterminated.

1985 The Year of Terror!

Based on his initial promise when he assumed power, Samuel Doe was supposed to relinquish power to a civilian government through the democratic process of election and voting. Since his popularity was at its lowest ebb, coupled with the suffering and dissatisfaction of the Liberian people, Samuel Doe knew that his days were numbered. However, with the support of his ethnic group and some sycophants who became wealthy through him, the 1985 election became a disaster; it was rigged in his favor. This was much to the disappointment of many, as it was clearly evident that Doe lacked both the intellectual capability and the administrative experience and competence to control the Ship of State.

A few months after Doe's infamous election, he re-instated himself as a civilian head of the government. Meanwhile, on November 12, 1985, due to the outcry of the masses, General Thomas Quiwonkpa, the second in command, staged a coup d'etat against Doe. General Quiwonkpa originated from the Gio ethnic group in Nimba County, northeastern Liberia. He was a very charismatic person who clearly opposed Doe's dictatorship and his un-ending grip to power.

Mysteriously, the coup attempt only lasted a few hours. General Quiwonkpa had promised on National television that he was not going to shed blood, but was going to remove Samuel Doe for betraying the trust of the Liberian people. During the initial successful hours of the coup, thousands of Liberians thronged the streets dancing and jubilating, and everything was video recorded!

Hours later, Doe's henchmen unfurled the attempted coup and Doe regained power.

Henceforth, Doe became monstrous, dangerous and deadly! General Quiwonkpa was quickly disposed of as Doe's elite and dedicated soldiers called SATU devoured the body of Quiwonkpa like men from the Stone Age. Doe's anger did not terminate with Quiwonkpa's death; he ordered more atrocities to be committed against the Nimba people where Quiwonkpa came from. His village was completely destroyed along with adjoining villages. According to the British Broadcast Corporation, Doe's soldiers also ravished Saniquellie, the capital of Nimba County: men, women and children were thrown alive into wells, their properties looted and destroyed.

In addition, many of the indigenes of Nimba County who were enlisted in the army were rounded up and secretly executed. Living conditions started getting worse in the country. It was the upsurge of terror! Anyone or even the press who dared say or print anything against the Doe's government was threatened with severe persecution or arson!

Although the sources of the Liberian conflict are complex, on one level, it represents an attempt by Americo-Liberians to re-establish themselves as the major political force in Liberia. The war was not about ethnic groups seeking dominance over each other. According to an article published by GlobalSecurity.Org, Charles Taylor led the invasion into Liberia in the name of trying to right the wrong for the Gios and Manos. This was the motivator for the two ethnic groups who joined the movement. When the Taylor rebels entered Nimba County their home, the conflict quickly drew in the Mandingoes, who are predominantly Muslims. The Gio ethnic group soon formed their own separate rebel forces under Prince Johnson, and a bloody three-way civil war began.

The Treacherous Incursion

In December 1989, rebel activities were more pronounced in the capital city of Monrovia. Local Newspapers and electronic media incessantly reported on rebel activities occurring elsewhere too, in the rural parts of Liberia and in Nimba County.

Alleged rebels caught by soldiers of the Armed Forces of Liberia (AFL) were paraded in front of television cameras and aired almost every day on the one and only television station, (ELTV—Channel 6).

"Tell the listening public all about your mission." A Military interviewer would say to one rebel prisoner.

"Yes sir!" he would reply. "My name is Sunday Gah. I'm from Grand Bassa County. I was looking for job, so one of my friends told me that Charles Taylor (Rebel Leader of the National Patriotic Front of Liberia who later dethroned Doe) was training some men in Burkina Faso. So I went in one plane with my friend. They carried us to one camp, and then they trained us for six weeks and gave us guns. But they did not tell us what to do …"

This was the order of the day as a new rebel is paraded before the television screen each night with a slightly varied version but similar story. Quite often, materials seized from these rebels would be displayed on the screen such as identification cards, red flags marked with the initials, N.P.F.L., ammunition etc. Ironically, this dangerous spectacle of events became the subject of amusement. Friends meeting at beer parlors would sit, drink, chat and laugh at the daily events of rebel stories on national television.

What did the Government do to arrest the situation? Doe commissioned several high ranking military officers assisted by a platoon of soldiers to go to the villages and stop the incursion. These men were given vehicles, equipment, per-diem and other logistics.

Rather than carry out their mission, these soldiers demanded to be treated as very important persons (V.I.P.) among the villagers. They ate all their live-stock and farm animals on a daily basis. To compensate for their presence, they would mete out all kinds of atrocities against the villagers—rape and the live burial of people in water wells. The village of the late General Quiwonkpa was burned to the ground leaving villagers fleeing in all directions for their dear lives. Even farms were destroyed and valuable goods looted. After a week or two, these soldiers would return to Monrovia looking very robust and showing off their pot bellies on television.

Despite all these, the incursion was never curbed. Rebel activities spread from Nimba to Buchanan, Grand Bassa County. A fierce battle ensued on the Buchanan-Monrovia highway. It was alleged that the AFL killed some rebels along with one of their leaders, a United States of America trained soldier, Sgt. Johnson. As consequence, some of the residents of Buchanan began to flee into Monrovia. Unfortunately, several of them were ambushed and killed on the highway.

Many more atrocities continued to be meted out to the people of Nimba County including those living in Monrovia. Newspapers reported some gruesome stories and showed pictures of mutilated bodies of Nimba citizens.

While this was going on, the Defense Minister, John Peter was languishing in jail. He was alleged to have been involved in the ritualistic murder of a cousin of President Doe.

Another Minister of Defense was quickly sworn in. He was General Brown, about 5' 9" tall, dark complexioned and approximately 60 years or older. Under his administration, there was very little or no security, things continued to deteriorate on a daily basis. Making matters worse, on National television, President Doe banned any press report on rebel activity whatsoever. Looking at General Brown, he said,

"Mr. Minister of Defense, if I as much as hear anyone mention the word 'rebel'—I order you to make cars available, that person will take us to where the rebel is …"

From that day on, news and reports on rebel activities were heavily censored by the Government agencies, especially the Ministry of Information, the major spokes organ of the Government. On numerous times, the Minister of Information, looking shrewd and stern would openly deny rebel incursion. At other times, he would say that the Government had everything under control and that people should go about their business normally and without fear.

This deteriorating state of affairs continued for a couple of months. Things got worse, local shops and stores were devoid of goods and groceries on their shelves. Rice, the staple food was not only exorbitantly expensive, but became quite scarce.

Regarding rebel activities, there was a total black-out of the print media.

Complacency In the state of Insecurity

It was as if the people of Monrovia were relying on Doe's government words, because up until the months of February and March 1990, people were complacently going about their businesses as if nothing was happening in the country.

However, Government Ministers who heard information from reliable sources did not take matters lightly. Many of them sold their houses and other properties, collected other loot and left the country under the pretence that they were attending international conferences and seminars. The Ministers of Foreign Affairs, Health, Transportation, Public Works, and many others abandoned their ships mid-stream and took flight.

Newspaper establishments who defied Doe's orders and dared mention rebel activities in their publications became the victims of arson. An example was the Daily Observer Newspaper Ltd. An article was published and the forbidden word—'rebel' was mentioned. The following day, fire gutted their establishment, destroyed their archives and thousands of dollars worth of printing equipment. Some of their staff was also man handled.

In the absence of news, things began to happen in Monrovia, awakening people to the reality of the state of danger they were in. A former Engineer at the Ministry of Public Works, Mr. T. Guy was brutally murdered.

The People Protest

By March 1990, things began to deteriorate at a geometric pace. Gasoline became scarce in addition to other commodities. Mobility by vehicles became a very expensive venture. The reality of the danger started dawning on helpless Liberians.

People began to seek spiritual resolution either to calm their frustrations or to obtain an instant miracle from God. Prayer services became the order of the day in Christian Churches and among prayer bands. The Centennial Pavilion, an exquisite hall formerly used for very important events like presidential inauguration was not spared as a praying ground. Usually after several songs and prayers, guest speakers who were bold enough would address problems on the political and social issues. They ended the services with a strong plea or warning to the Government.

Newspapers again resurfaced, leaflets circulated, and in some, the resignation of Doe was demanded.

All these culminated into the people's protest. After a prayer service at the S. Trowen Nagbe Methodist Church, staff from various institutions such as hospitals, schools and government offices began a long march to the American Embassy in Mamba Point. People carried all sorts of banners and placards. On some of them, people sought the intervention of our super power friend, the United States of America. Upon reaching the Embassy grounds, a statement was read by a Liberian representative who pleaded for the help of the American Government.

At that time, the U.S. Government had about 2000 marines on alert in ships docked just off the Liberian coast. Later on, it was alleged that the marines were there to safeguard the lives of the American residents and staff who worked in the embassy. The U.S. Ambassador had been recalled and there was no replacement for several months.

It was the U.S. Charge d' Affaire who met and responded to the huge crowd standing in front of the Embassy. In essence, his response was that the situation was an internal affair and that "… these are Liberians killing Liberians." Our beacon of hope was dashed; the worst was yet to come!

The Un-Relinquishing Pharaoh

Meanwhile, S.K. Doe did not seem to realize he was loosing his grip on power. Almost on a daily basis, there were protest marches coupled with the lack of food and basic commodities. Government machineries and institutions were non-functional and had collapsed. The so-called Government Ministers had abandoned their posts. Those who had looted government's coffers for years untouched carted their loot overseas. These writings on the wall were either not bold enough for Doe to read or he was such an illiterate he could not read!

S.K. Doe would not budge! He made frantic and desperate moves to control the country with force and brutality. His Special Anti Terrorist Unit (SATU) came into notoriety and committed all sorts of wickedness against the Liberian people especially those from Nimba County.

The Emergence of Refugees

Things continued to take a nose dive in Liberia. By May 1990, the United Nations office premises became a refuge ground for thousands of Liberians, more notably indigenes from Nimba County. They became the hunted, the molested and were deprived of everything but the breath that was still in them.

On the morning of May 31, 1990, blood marks were seen on the walls of the United Nations office in Sinkor, Monrovia. It was the long awaited spark needed to trigger a reaction. It was alleged that someone was murdered, but there was no evidence of a corpse. This incident became the premise upon which the United Nations office was closed down in Liberia on that same day. Accordingly, the act was a violation of the United Nations Charter.

It promulgated the evacuation of all non-essential foreign staff of the United Nations office. Only core foreign staff remained such as the Resident Representative, the Deputy Representative and the Administrative Officer. The U.N. office was in a state of security alert! Four senior local officers including myself were given walkie-talkies (subsequently a death device) and were told to stay at our respective homes. A chartered plane came from neighboring Guinea and took away the remaining foreign staff, leaving the rest of the locally recruited ones at the mercy of the ensuing war.

Thousands who sought refuge on the grounds of the United Nations saw their hope for survival dashed to pieces with the sudden closure of the U.N. office! In a state of panic, some of the refugees fled to churches, others sought refuge in school buildings and still others found their way to the few Red Cross offices available.

The atrocities and horror stories that were often heard that occurred in Nimba County, began to surface in Monrovia. The British Broadcasting corporation reported that hundreds of people, mostly Gio and Mano tribes who sought refuge in the Lutheran Church building on 12th Street were reportedly massacred in cold blood!

The scene was horrific!! Mothers with their babies on their backs clamoring to escape through the Church windows were gunned down with tons of bullets, sparing neither mother nor child. Even pregnant women were also killed including people who were already asleep. The Church building became a pool of blood of innocent victims.

Who were the perpetrators of such wicked, demonic and savagery act? Some alleged they were done by S.K. Doe's soldiers. How did they disguised themselves and entered the Church premises? What was the motive for targeting mostly women, children and babies?

Others alleged the act was carried out by the NPFL rebels, some of whom were Gio and Mano with the sole intention of defaming the already notorious Doe. Only heavens knew what the true story was.

For the residents of Monrovia, the massacre at the Lutheran Church became an eye-opener to the reality of the danger that was present. Things continued to deteriorate on a daily basis. The month of June 1990, was filled with news of deaths. On June 10, 1990, three prominent Liberians, Vanjah Richards, Coleman and Ricks from the small town of Clay-Ashland were grotesquely murdered.

The following section depicts my daily notes written at home. They represent the daily trials that my family and I encountered in the hands of rebels before our great escape.

Section Two:
Daily Dairy

The Month of June, 1990

Wednesday, June 6

At about 8:30 a.m., my husband and I were dressed for town. He wanted to check his office for telex messages and I wanted to see my brother, David, who worked with the National Bank of Liberia. We had never been in town since the U.N. office was closed on May 31, 1990. As we drove down the road, my uncle's wife who was just living next door to us in Brewerville, along with her children, were beckoning us to go back home. They yelled that soldiers were all over Brewerville. However, we decided to drive as far as the check point, and if we encountered any difficulty, we would return home to our three sons.

On our way, we met Rev. J. Walker who stopped to talk to us briefly. We drove as far as the Lott Carey School. We noticed that there weren't any cars on the streets. A fully armed soldier passed by us. He gave us a vicious look but never said a word. I told my husband, 'lets go back home!' Immediately, he made a 'U' turn and headed home. Again, we saw the same soldier coming straight at us. My husband just kept driving. We felt God's divine presence was with us because the soldier didn't bother us.

When we almost reached home, right in front of the late Representative Curtis' house, we saw about six or seven soldiers with boxes of ammunition being divided among them. Quickly, one of them ran to us. "Hold it! Get out of the car and open your trunk!" He demanded.

I felt panic and fear! My husband got down and said, "we live right there around the corner."

"I know you, I know you very well, go back to your car and stay home,—this place is off limits!" The soldier yelled back.

My husband got back in the car and sped quickly home. We were terribly shaken. We didn't utter a word to each other until we entered our house. We stayed locked indoors and were mostly on our knees praying. On the previous night, I couldn't sleep, we heard shooting all around us. We thought it was just at the checkpoint, some few miles from our residence. If we had known that soldiers were already in Brewerville, we wouldn't have risked venturing to go to town today.

Later on today, my brother David who lived in Lakpasi came to Brewerville to see us. He was afraid of all the gruesome stories and rumors being spread all over the city. He met us looking very frightened but still in one piece.

Sunday, June 10

Every day, from sunrise to sunset, we constantly lived in fear. The fear of not knowing what was going to happen next. It was almost getting dark today when our neighbor's boyfriend Jockey, came knocking frantically on our front door. When we opened the door, he was standing there trembling. He said some people had just killed Clay Ashland's mayor, Mr. Vanjah Richards and two other residents. Mr. Richards was a very good sculptor. He taught techniques of this art at the University of Liberia. What a waste! We were stunned! We didn't know who did it. We didn't know if they were going from house to house killing people!

Tuesday, June 12

It's almost two weeks since the closure of the U.N. Office on May 31, 1990. It seemed like two years of both mental and physical torture! We are always locked in, too afraid to play or work in our big yard; afraid of being hit by stray bullets or being molested by any group of drunken, drugged, undisciplined men in uniforms.

Our children's school, Hilton Van Ee, was forced to close down today. We dared not go out to obtain their progress report. I remembered the motto of the school quite vividly. It states: "If you think education is expensive, try ignorance."

We can certainly see what ignorance and lack of foresight in leadership can do-put the nation and its people in peril! Our three boys ages 10, 7, and 6 years cannot go outdoors to play. We lived this torture day by day!!!

Wednesday, June 13

A State of anarchy is in the making. Nobody seems or feels safe in the country anymore. A delegation of Nigerians met the Foreign Minister, to complain about threats to their people by a group of 'concerned Liberians'.

Later on today, a make-shift funeral rite is being carried out for the three prominent Clay Ashland citizens who were savagely murdered a couple of days ago. It is being broadcasted by the local television station. Three gray coffins lay side by side. They contained the remains of V. Richards, Coleman and Ricks respectively. Several men and women were seen weeping and wailing. The rites were performed by the late Bishop Brown. Their remains were buried in sandy graves; no tombs, just plain red sand!!

Thursday, June 14

At about 9:30 a.m., many Liberians converged on the grounds of the United Methodist Church in Sinkor to stage a 'peace walk'. They included people from all works of life: teachers, doctors, nurses, students, blue collar workers, and market men and women. It was intended for the restoration of peace and the condemnation of the rampant killings of Gio, Mano, Mandingo, Krahn and Congo people.

This was one of many signs that Doe paid no heed to. What ever the representatives said or presented, fell on deaf ears. Simply put, Doe just didn't care; rather, he became more ruthless.

Friday, June 15

Today, the Economic Commission of West African States (E.C.O.W.A.S) and the Organization of African Unity (O.A.U) sent representatives to negotiate a peace treaty with Liberia's warring factions.

According to the British Broadcasting Corporation (BBC), there was a complete deadlock on the peace talks between the two warring parties, namely, the Government Force of S.K. Doe and the Rebel Group of the National Patriotic Front headed by Charles Taylor. The talks were being held in Freetown, Sierra-Leone. They only concurred to a joint cease fire agreement signed by both parties.

There has been no tangible statement from the National Patriotic Front. Later in the day, the BBC reported that Charles Taylor had threatened to attack Monrovia in twelve hours if there was no resolution from the peace talks.

Wednesday, June 20

The Voice of America (VOA) radio quoted the French News Agency about the resignation of two Liberian Ministers—the Finance Minister and the Foreign Affairs Minister. About a week ago, the Director of Police had also resigned.

Two, three at a time, or more, ministers abandoned their posts and left government institutions non-operational.

Monday, June 25

Today marked the scheduled peace-talks. It was the final talk between the two opposing forces. We were hopefully anticipating some positive news that would get us out of this quagmire we're in.

At about 4:15p.m., BBC announced that the talks never took place due to the absence of the NPFL. We were heartbroken by the news.

"Not again!" My husband shouted in disappointment.

Few hours later today, the spokesman for the NPFL, Tom Wonyewuh said they were not going to waste their time and money to attend the talks except President Doe resigns. He said they've constituted their own government and their officials would come to power in a couple of days.

"You mean this thing is not going to be over and our lives will just dwindle away?" My husband muttered in frustration after listening to the news.

Meanwhile, the Rebel Front had captured Careysburg and the University of Liberia's Fendell Campus, about fifteen miles from the capital, Monrovia.

President Doe's jet which cost about $22 million has been seized in Great Britain by the British government. This is due to the debt lawsuits filed against the Liberian Government. One was for $20 million owed for gasoline given to the National Petroleum and Refinery Company (N.P.R.C), and the other for something else. Since the total cost exceeded the cost of the plane, another government property is expected to be seized. The plane was captured when it took members of Doe's family to England as they fled the trouble back home.

Wednesday, June 27

Today, various professional groups, lawyers, teachers and students marched again to the Capitol building to present a statement to President Doe. The essence of the statement was to demand his resignation in view of the deterioration of living conditions in Liberia. The march was unsuccessful because it was the same day that Doe decided to terminate the life of one Private Grear. He was found guilty of murdering one Wrimonga. So as the marchers arrived at the B.T.C (Barclay Training Center), soldiers fired in the air for several hours. There were reports that some shots were fired into the crowd and at moving vehicles. Some of these protesters fell to the ground and were trampled on. The incident was never reported by the local news stations.

Friday, June 29

Our small battery-operated transmission radio has been our only communication link to the outside world. Everyday, we listened attentively for any word of a breakthrough. The dial has been permanently set on the frequency of the British Broadcasting Corporation.

Today, the B.B.C. reported that the Rebels have taken over the hydro plant at the White Plains. As the result, there hasn't been a single drop of pipe-borne water in Monrovia since Wednesday night!

At about 8:45 p.m., the flow of electricity also stopped. The five pieces of fish, pepper and some food stuff I had in the refrigerator were on the verge of getting rotten.

Worse still, my family and I did not sleep last night! There was shooting all night long! We felt entrapped.

The Month of July

Monday, July 2

This is the fourth day we are without electricity!

Despite the intense darkness, we managed to get about 3-4 hours of sleep last night. God helped us to wake up in one piece. Around 8:30a.m., to our horror and dismay, we heard shelling and bombing. The horrible sounds came from the north, the direction of either Clay-Ashland or Caldwell. It went on for several hours!

My husband and I became so frightened that we decided to pack a few of our things and get the children ready for any emergency flight.

At 2 p.m., just as I had finished writing in my diary, I lay on the bed to get some rest. Suddenly! I heard gunshots very close by. I ran quickly to our children's room, got them out of their beds to the corridor and down on the floor we lay. I was lying in the center with one child on the left and two on my right.

I thought about my husband, but couldn't get to the bedroom where he was. As a matter of fact, we didn't have any time to move!

All at once, we could hear singing of tribal songs by a group of people and then the attack was on our house! These people were in our yard shooting machine guns all over our house! There were two heavy artillery shelling that sounded like bombs. I thought our house was collapsing on us!! I was on the floor with our children and started yelling "Jesus, Jesus!"

Our oldest son started crying.

I tell you, the firing was so heavy and intense. I heard my husband crying in the bathroom-

"We beg you, we beg you."

As I was lying in the hallway with the children, I heard things like bullets dropping inside our house. I thought and said to myself, Lord; the people are inside our house!!

But thank God, they weren't! The shooting lasted for about ten horrific minutes!

Afterwards, it all subsided and they left.

We were too frightened to get up from the floor. My husband crawled out of the bedroom to find out how we were. Thank God, we were all in one piece! I thought for a while that we were in heaven.

The shooting and shelling continued in our neighborhood for a long time.

My gracious Lord! I have never experienced anything like this in all my 36years on earth! We were so afraid that we all slept in the hallway that night and two subsequent nights there after—two horrible sleepless nights!

Tuesday, July 3

Today, there has been no attack, but the shooting and shelling around us were so intense and loud that we heard and felt the vibrations in every part of our home.

At about 11 a.m., my uncle sent his wife and two of their daughters to find out how we were. When they came, we were still lying in the hall way, too scared to even go to the door! It seemed as if God had sent them to cheer us a little. Their presence gave us the boldness to get outside of the house, quickly fetched some well water and disposed of the rotten food that was attracting driver ants into the house.

During the heavy shelling yesterday, my husband and I decided that we were going to move to the Voice of America's Compound (V.O.A) just a few kilometers from where we lived. We just couldn't bear it anymore!

Wednesday, July 4

At 7 a.m., on the BBC, we heard that President Doe had agreed to resign! We started praising God immediately!

We looked out the window and spoke to our neighbor, Olivia. She and her only son were alright.

Daniel our house help went outside to make fire and heat some water and we were able to bathe for the first time in three days.

In the evening, we heard on the radio that the ECOWAS team and seven African representatives were going to Freetown to bring final peace to Liberia tomorrow, July 5.

"Lord, God, we beg you, please bring this conflict to a peaceful end by tomorrow."

Thursday, July 5

Our hope has been dashed on this day because the ECOWAS meeting could not convene due to the absence of some key leaders.

We continued to stay indoors. By this time, we were running short on food. I have only a quarter bag of rice, few cans of mackerel fish, and some margarine remaining. We reduced the frequency of our meals and only eat once a day mainly in the afternoon. Everybody has started loosing weight!

I felt so sorry for my sons, so sorry that we are caught in this mess.

Friday, July 6

The ECOWAS meeting could not convene again due to the absence of the National Patriotic Front Representatives.

We heard of some more destruction in town. Some parts of New Kru Town and the Coast Guard Base were severely bombarded.

BBC reported that the NPFL has reached Central Monrovia and has attacked the Executive Mansion where the President lives. However, there was a counter attack by the Government Forces and the NPFL withdrew 2.5 miles away.

Saturday, July 7

President Doe announced a cease-fire on the part of government troops. The government's radio station, ELBS, came on for few minutes to make the presidential announcement and then went off the air again. There was no response from the Rebels, so, we were able to sleep a little quietly on Saturday night.

Sunday, July 8

At 5 p.m., during the BBC broadcast, Thomas Wonyewuh the NPFL Rebel Spokesman announced the rejection of the Government's cease-fire. But he promised that they would be at the Peace-talks in Freetown, on Tuesday, July 10. We felt a little sigh of relief at this piece of news but weren't very sure if they were going to keep their words or not.

One would wonder why we remained trapped in the country and didn't escape during the mass exodus of people that fled earlier. We had seen two coup d'etats, but none of them engaged the masses of the people. So, we thought this was going to be like another coup and a new government would just come to power. We had no prior knowledge of the ammunitions, manpower and logistics being gathered by Charles Taylor to plunge the country into a bloody fratricidal war! Those who were privileged with this information had already left.

Tuesday, July 10

At about 7:20 a.m., electricity is being restored! We were all so amazed that my youngest son Arnold shouted, "Mammy, its magic!"

This is also the day of the agreed Peace-talks to be held in Freetown.

We pray and hope something tangible emanates from the talks.

Sunday, July 15

As I was praying sometime last week, God impressed two dates on my mind—the 14th and the 20th. So I expected a great miracle on the 14th. Friday the 13th was a very dull day, so, I was really looking forward to a miracle on the 14th.

Saturday the fourteenth came, I was hoping that God would either provide a means for my family to escape from Liberia or bring the war to a cessation. Nothing happened! Rather, the day has been relatively calm and we spent the day as usual in fear—: children shouldn't talk aloud, laugh or even play. We quickly scrambled up something to eat and found our way to bed. God took us through the night but we could hear heavy shooting all night long. We couldn't sleep.

On Sunday the 15th, we decided we couldn't bear the fear and shooting any longer. So we planned to move to the VOA compound. We prayed, and told our neighbor our intention. They discouraged us with more frightful stories especially the recent killings in Caldwell, a distance not too far from our residence. But when I told my uncle's wife, she immediately encouraged us to move. Without hesitating not even for a second, we packed a few of our belongings and got in our car. We also took some of my uncle's children along.

My husband started the car, it just wouldn't start! We were in the yard for about 45 minutes pushing and trying to repair the car. Everybody began to sweat in panic! My husband said, "Maybe God doesn't want us to go."

I was adamant. My uncle's wife helped us to get a mechanic who got the car started. We headed to VOA.

On our way, at about 30 yards from our house, was a check-point manned by two savage looking government soldiers. My husband gave them $1.00 and they allowed us to go through.

Brewerville looked like a ghost town! All the houses on both sides of the road were bare of occupants! It was then that we realized the magnitude of the danger we were in.

Finally, we reached the VOA's compound. We were fortunate to see our old friends, Mr. and Mrs. Attah. They gave us a small room in their 3-bedroom unit. It was empty, nothing to sleep on but the bare floor. We were very happy to sleep on the floor, just anything, so long as we were away from all that shooting and shelling.

For the first time in weeks, we were able to sleep for few hours. The company of other people around us gave us some assurance and some sense of security.

Tuesday, July 17

Our oldest son Marvin has contacted malaria. He has been vomiting, weak, no appetite and has a temperature of 104 degrees. "Lord, I don't know what to do anymore." There is a Red Cross booth located in the compound but there is hardly any good medication still remaining! All I could do was put a wet towel on his forehead to keep him cool. I scrambled around in the compound begging people for any available malaria medicine. I got some tablets and gave them to him.

I knew it wasn't sufficient to cure him, but it would alleviate his distress.

"Lord, how and when do we get out of all these pains and sufferings?"

The final peace talks scheduled for today is postponed again due to the absence of the concerned parties.

Thursday, July 19

Final peace-talks are abandoned, the NPFL left and could not reach consensus with the ECOWAS group. No cease fire!

Friday, July 20

On this day, there is very heavy bombing all throughout the day and night. Missiles were fired from the Executive Mansion indiscriminately to Duala, New Krutown. You name it! The fire works and vibrations could be seen and felt where we are! "Lord have mercy!"

Saturday, July 21

The Bowden Delegation, who represented President Doe's Government at the Peace Talks, suggested over BBC News that President Doe should resign as a meaningful sacrifice for peace and should turn the government to a nationally broad base one. The suggestion was sanctioned by the ECOWAS group.

We were anxiously waiting that Doe would exercise some degree of intelligence and comply with the group.

Sunday, July 22

President Doe announced over BBC via telex message that he regretted the decision of the ECOWAS and that he was going to maintain the constitution of Liberia; he was not going to resign but would fight until the last man dies. "Lord, please save us from this demon and lunatic called Doe."

Friday, July 27

At about 7:00 p.m., I heard people screaming and running all over the VOA Refugee camp where we were residing. I panicked and thought Government soldiers had entered the camp to kill us! But as God would have it, it was the ELWA Radio Station that resumed broadcasting after been silent for over three weeks. The NPFL Rebel Leader Charles Taylor was on the air announcing the dissolution of President Doe's government and cabinet. He promised a new election in six months' time.

Some people in the camp were jubilant expressing joy that their ordeal was over and a new government was coming into power.

My family and I were rather cautious about showing any emotions, not knowing what to expect.

Saturday, July 28

As we listened to the BBC broadcast today, it was reported that the American Government denies or doubts the dissolution of the Doe's Government. It was further reiterated that there has been no change in the Executive Mansion, home of the president since the announcement by one of the Rebel leaders.

I could not believe my ears. I thought for a moment. "What is the meaning of all this? Are they not cognizant of the persecution, hunger, thirst, sickness and pains suffered by hundreds of thousands of Liberians and foreigners that are trapped in this City?"

Many more are being brutally massacred every day! I started talking to myself, "Don't they want this nightmare and horror we are experiencing to stop? Who established the Doe's government? Are they not watching the atrocities he and his henchmen are committing on the people of this nation?

Lord! Please help us."

Monday, July 30

Listening to the BBC has become a daily ritual for us. In today's broadcast, at about 2:00a.m., it was reported that Doe's men (from the Krahn tribe), stormed the Lutheran Church in Sinkor, Monrovia and killed at least 600 people, mostly women and children!! Some of the women's heads were battered with bullets while their babies were still tied on their backs. These women were killed as they were climbing the Church's windows to escape!

"What cruelty? What a disregard and sacrilege for God's House of worship?" I screamed!

ELWA Radio Station was also destroyed by Doe's Force.

"What a shame?" Monrovia Streets are littered with dead bodies of civilians.

Meanwhile, two Krahn women were caught at the Brewerville Checkpoint carrying grenades in their underwear. They were destined for the VOA camp where thousands were seeking refuge. Lord save us from the hands of demons!

In the mean time, a friction existed between Charles Taylor and his deputy, Prince Johnson; each publicly denounced and condemned the other.

We didn't know what to make of all these. When we thought things were reaching an end, we continued to hear confusing news as the country digressed into a state of anarchy.

The Month of August

Wednesday, August 1

Today marked the beginning of a new month. Most people in the compound fasted and prayed for God to give us a breakthrough. Ironically, there was hardly any food around. Sometimes, we looked desperately in the surrounding bushes around us for birds, ground hogs, any wild life that we could use as food, but they all disappeared. We just lived on wild vegetables that we could find around. This was often supplemented with palm kernels. Yet, people were willing to deny themselves of this meager food and fast for some miracle.

"Lord, please help us in this our state of horror and dilemma, we need a miracle of deliverance."

Sunday, August 5

Today marked the third week or our third Sunday at the VOA compound. At about 9 a.m., we woke up to the sound of war helicopters flying so low over the tops of the roofs. News got out quickly; the Americans at the Base are being evacuated and are no longer responsible for thousands of people who have taken refuge in their premises! At the same time, we also heard some so-called freedom fighters were shooting at the helicopters.

Pandemonium broke loose! Everybody started running from the Base! The children and I almost reached the main gate, when we saw some people running back. So, we too ran back to the house.

That night I couldn't sleep. I had bad dreams and nightmare—I envisioned a figure of my head, eyes shut, and sweats of blood running from the sides of my forehead.

In order to make matters worse, my husband became sick with malaria. He was of no help. He had taken 5 chloroquine tablets and was lying on the cold floor. I felt a sudden pang of fear and helplessness! Anyway, we packed our few belongings and managed to follow the thousands of people fleeing the VOA premises. Some of these people decided to trek to Freetown, Sierra-Leone. We were faced with a dilemma, should we join the thousands of people trekking or should we go back to our house?

I thought deeply; with a sick husband, three little boys, no food and water, we would be too weak to walk thousands of miles. Definitely, some of my family members will die on the road. Worse still, we have also heard stories of rebels who attacked refugees on the road, stole their possessions, raped the women and kill the men.

I expressed my thoughts and fears to my husband and together, we made the decision to go back to our house and await some great miracle through the OAU leaders' intervention on tomorrow, August 6th.

Thursday, August 9

Today, my entire family and I are in the Faith Baptist Church, which is about three miles from our home in Brewerville.

We fled our home yesterday, when we heard that residents of Brewerville were told to move out of their homes because Prince Johnson and Charles Taylor rebel factions were going to battle it out in Brewerville.

We all rushed in the car, valise, bags, pots etc. along with my uncle's children. A neighbor advised that it was dangerous to take our car. So, we all started walking with our belongings on our heads on that rainy Wednesday afternoon. We walked for over an hour. My husband and our children were in front, while my uncle's children, Agnes, Ruth and I trailed behind with our heavy loads.

We spent two days and nights in the church, lying on the cold floor with no toilet facility. We had no food but just lived on sugar cane that we up rooted by the road side and water!

On Wednesday night, our first night at the church, many people slept there. However, on the second night, only three families including us remained there. We were afraid to leave due to possible retaliation from Doe's troops. Rumor had it that President Doe was going to send his troops to destroy some of the settlements, with the suspicion that Charles Taylor's Front was there. We also heard from passers-by that fighting would be quite heavy in Brewerville on Wednesday night. Therefore, we decided to stay put in the church begging for God's protection until the next day August 10, before making an attempt to go back home.

Friday, August 10

"Praise God, Alleluia!" The Ghanaian contingent of the ECOWAS Peace-Keeping Force left Ghana for Freetown on August 9, with a force of about 2000 men. This contingent was headed by a Gen. Quainoo, nick-named 'Buffalo Soldier'.

Meanwhile, President Doe claimed an assassination attempt was made on his life. He said while he and Jacob Joe were sitting on the terrace of the Executive Mansion, an American Helicopter flew over and fired shots at them, but only Jacob Joe got wounded. How true and reliable this story is could not be validated. We have heard varied versions of Doe's accusations.

We really don't know what to believe any more.

Sunday, August 12

We hurriedly left our home for the third time due to heavy fighting in the area. We left for Korkor's village, about 10 miles from our home. Korkor Village is located on the Suehn High Way. During normal times, the village consisted of less than five hundred inhabitants and was headed by a chief. They were usually self-sufficient by growing their own food and raising life-stock. The village was densely covered with tall grass and trees. We felt an eerie feeling in the air as we walked the narrow foot-path leading to it.

Shooting was intense behind us as we trekked quickly. We got to the village by late evening; every square foot of ground space was covered by hundreds of people taking refuge there.

My husband's fluency in the local ethnic language 'Bassa', gave our family the opportunity to sleep in one of the rooms belonging to the village chief. The room was quite small, about ten feet by five feet. It had one tiny window. The inner part of the room was quite congested with all the chief's belongings. We hardly had space to move around. We couldn't even lie down. We spread some cloth on the clay floor for our sons to sleep while my husband and I sat up throughout the whole night. I thought to myself, 'we are really suffering! Lord, what have we done to deserve all these?' We had once risen from such life and God knows how we worked our way to the little comforts we had. Now, we have fled our home looking for safety in every nook and corner.

Tuesday, August 14

Monday was very gloomy. It rained throughout the day. Shooting could be heard in the little village from mid afternoon and all through the night.

Today, I thought we were going to wake up into some quietude; rather, it became a period of intense shooting and blasting. I couldn't bear to sit in the village kitchen where I was preparing our meal with fire wood. The ordeal sounded as if it was coming from Ricks Institute Junior College, about a few miles from the village. I was so afraid and confused and didn't know what to do anymore.

Everywhere we sought refuge seemed to accommodate us temporarily before all hell broke loose.

There was hardly any facility in the village; no water wells, no indoor toilets or even an out house. Every one of us had to use the bush. It was a nasty, horrible scene with feces all over the place. I felt sick and horrible. For the past 48 hours we've spent in the village, my family and I used the creek water for bathing and cooking. I was so afraid we were going to catch some kind of water-borne diseases like cholera, typhoid or dysentery. God really protected us.

Friday, August 17

Today, I'm writing about our experience at Korkor's village. On Wednesday August 15, at about 10 a.m., we had an encounter with some of Charles Taylor's rebels. They were five in number with one Melish as their Commander.

I was in the village kitchen cooking some rice, when suddenly, I saw armed men in colored clothes moving between the huts. One of them was wearing a cowboy's hat. As he passed by the kitchen, he greeted me. Then, all of a sudden, everybody was summoned to appear at the palava hut.

We assembled, leaving our terrified children behind. My husband and I sat separately. We tried to be calm and listened to Commander Melish as he intimidated us with all kinds of frightful talks. At the end, he told the village chief to have his people gather as many livestock as possible. He needed the food for his 150 rebels who would soon be in ambush.

Some villagers showed reluctance towards this new mandate. Immediately, one of the armed men stepped out in front of the group and fired in the air. One woman with a weak spell started trembling as if she was going to have a heart attack. She was told to leave.

Everybody dispersed quickly to find the livestock—goats, chickens and ducks that roamed about the village.

The armed man with the cowboy's hat called Saye singled out my husband.

"I want to see you," he said. He asked my husband all sorts of questions such as:

> "What's your tribe?"
> "What's your name?"
> "Where do you live?"
> "Where do you work?"
> "Where is the town house you live in?"

Saye even called Melish to the interrogation. My husband spoke his ethnic tongue Bassa. As God would have it, Melish was Bassa and Saye was Mano. All in all, the conversation was cordial, but Saye looked very mean and desperate. About an hour later, they freed my husband.

After the rebel group left with the people's ducks, chickens and sheep, my family and I quickly packed our things, never bothered to eat and fled. God guided us through the two miles walk in the bush until we got on the main road.

During our encounter at the village, when one of the rebels shot in the air, my youngest son who was left behind started crying, he thought they had shot us his parents.

Saturday, August 18

Today as we returned home, we heard that the same rebels, Saye, Melish and their accomplices went back to Korkor's village. This time around, they ordered all the people to bring out their belongings out in the open. They searched them and took all their valuables. It was told that a man had $900; the rebels took $800 and left only $100.00 with him. So-called freedom fighters, nothing but a den of thieves!

At about 6p.m., three rag-tags looking rebels or so called freedom fighters came to our yard. I was in the bathroom and as soon as I looked out the window, I glimpsed at one of them just roaming about! I became confused and terrified! Suddenly, I heard my husband yelled, "we here oh!!" He ran outside and met the two men, the third, the commander came later. I put on my clothes quickly and hid by the living room window, watching everything that was going on.

Frisky, one of our two dogs started barking fiercely. It was quite annoying to the rebels and a member of the group threatened to kill the poor dog! What kind of savages are these?

These men looked very fearful. Some of them were dressed in black pants and shirts and wore women's wigs. Others wore women's hats and clothes and had their AK-47 guns strapped across their chests along with dozens of magazines.

The commander joined the rest of his men later. As soon as he arrived, he started to interrogate my husband. He asked various questions about his name, tribe, place of work, etc. Afterwards, he began the intimidation streak-

"You teach at the University of Liberia that means you are working for President Doe's government. You are one of the ones that gave Doe his degree ..."

My husband tried his best to explain to these functional literates that when one teaches at the university, doesn't necessarily mean one works for the president. The sequel to all that was the car issue.

"We need this car for about two days," demanded the commander.

Meanwhile, I was in the house standing by the window listening to the interrogation. I beefed up courage and stepped outside. I was terrified but steady, so together with my husband, we started begging these men. My husband spoke Bassa to them. One of the three called Innis claimed he knew my husband's relatives in River Cess.

We gave them $5.00 for their cigarettes. We kept giving them what little money we have left for fear that if we didn't, they would kill us and still take the money anyway. God touched their hearts and they left.

Sunday, August 19

Every Sunday now seemed memorable in our lives. At about 4 p.m., two rebels were once more in our yard! Innis and another new one called William. They demanded the car again. This time, they walked right into our dining room. All of us sat down along with our children, terrified as usual. We started begging them again to spare the car.

Then they asked for money, we had very little left, so we gave them $10.00.

Just in that time, Innis, who was standing outside, walked in with his gun.

"This man not for us, let's take that car!" He shouted.

This is the so-called River Cess man! All at once, William bounced up, "my man, you right!"

He left the $10.00 on the table and the two of them went outside to take another look at the car.

In an impromptu manner, William declared,

"The only way I would leave this car, is except you people give me $50.00." He had earlier asked my husband for some rice.

So once more, we started begging them again. Finally, William asked for the $10.00 we initially offered and then both of them left. They even advised us to take the engine and tires down. In other words, they told us to demobilize the car. We were very cynical about their advice.

However, my husband went ahead and removed the car's rotor and four tires. I became so fed up with all these harassments that I put God to the test. I spoke to the Lord and said—"God, will you allow your children to be harassed, intimidated and our lives at stake in the hands of Satan's Children?

Lord you know best!"

Our hearts and minds were so hardened that we decided to put all the parts back on the car. If they should come the next day, they can take the car away and let all damnation, God's wrath, and all our labor and pains go with them!!

Before I forget, it was the same Saturday, August 18, 1989, early in the morning that my husband accepted the Lord and became a born-again Christian! You know Lord; you cannot make us ashamed after such a glorious occasion!

Tuesday, August 21

To God be the glory! Monday, August 20, was a rather peaceful day for us—no visitation, no molestation, God is faithful!

But today is the D-day for us! Three visits! with complete harassment, intimidation etc, that I pray never to experience anything like this again in my life.

At about 11:30a.m., the first group of so-called freedom fighters came consisting of the Bassa commander along with six other men. Their visit although frightened us, was rather cordial and friendly. The commander said they just passed by to greet. He asked for things like food stuff and money, but we had nothing to give, so they left.

At about 3:30p.m., the dog alarmed us of the presence of the second group of about ten men. This group looked fierce and deadly. They held machine guns, knives and long sharp swords!

The leader, Hemson stood in the yard and yelled out my husband's name!

My husband ran outside and I was right behind him. The sight was cruel and frightening! My husband started crying. Straightaway, they started to abuse him.

"What kind of man is this, you some kind of damn woman with f ... p ... h ...? They took him to the living room porch and I followed.

"You go back inside", one of them shouted at me. "We want only the man." I went back in the house, told the children to go to our room, while I listened nearby as they interrogated my husband. They asked all sorts of intimidating questions-

How he worked for Doe, they even threatened to kill him along with two other NDPL men—Solomon Walker and another fellow.

Next thing I heard, somebody said, "Let all the people in the house get outside!" I ran and got our three sons and my young niece Agnes who was spending some time with the family. Our second son was sick with malaria. It was pouring rain on that day. We all lined up under the rain. One of the armed men came by us and clicked his machine gun and a bullet fell right by my foot!!

"So, these are all your children?" Hemson asked. I responded in the affirmative, not knowing what they were going to do next.

"Let the woman and the children go back inside," he declared. Immediately, I held the boys' hands and we ran into the house.

My husband and our house help Daniel remained outside on the porch. The interrogation and intimidation continued. After Hemson finished, the awfully scary-looking one called Lamin became the next interrogator while Hemson moved towards our kitchen. I had locked the kitchen door when I came in with the kids.

"Who locked this door?" yelled Hemson. "You don't lock the door or else I shoot everyone in here!" he shouted.

With trembling hands, I opened the door as he entered with his machine gun and sword. He looked all around, then went back outside and summoned four of his men into our home. The new issue was arms. They alleged that we have arms and ammunition. The logic is that my husband taught at the University, so he must have guns. As a consequence, they were going to search our home thoroughly and if any gun is found, they were going to kill everyone in the family declared Hemson.

All of a sudden, my husband became very courageous, he called Hemson aside and said, "Look, we don't have any gun here, please promise me that none of your men would plant a gun in this house." Hemson promised that he and his men won't do that.

The search began, from the guest room, under our mattresses, side cup-board drawers, everywhere and everything.

As we went from room to room in the five bedroom house, one of the armed men started talking some nonsense talk to me. "Go bring the money and rice you have hidden, you all just here enjoying while we there suffering in the bush." He saw my $10.00 in one of the cup-boards and grabbed it. The commander saw him and was told to put it back.

The last room they entered was our bedroom. As soon as they entered, the first place they looked, was behind the door! Remembering some days back, I had placed the walkie-talkie given to the senior staff of the United Nations in an open carton right behind our bedroom door. One day, my husband questioned me about the whereabouts of the walkie-talkie. I told him where it was. He took it and threw it in the ceiling. He must have had some intuition that the device may cost us our lives!

The Episode of the Walkie-Talkie

Before the United Nations office in Monrovia closed in May, we had a security drill by some officials of the Security Council from New York. They came specifically to perform the drill. At the end, the senior staff which consisted of about five locally recruited Program Officers including myself and Ben P. was given walkie-talkies with derived code names to be used when the United Nations office closes.

As novices, we gladly received the 'death device' and never gave a second thought about its usefulness in a heated escalating war which was composed of child soldiers. Most of the children used by Charles Taylor were not only uneducated but were drugged and knew nothing about the Geneva Conventions on war!

We should have known that nobody was going to rescue the National officers because as tension mounted, all the international officers and their families were evacuated in specially chartered planes leaving us the nationals at the mercy and perils of the rag-tag soldiers.

Earlier on, God had given me a sign about the danger of the walkie-talkie, but I didn't pay any heed. I remembered when we had electricity; I used to place the walkie-talkie in the kitchen pantry to be charged.

One day, I took it off the charger and decided to call Ben P. whose code name was 'Music'. I was wearing a gold chain on my neck then.

"Music, Music, this is 'Score' calling."

All of a sudden, the lead magnet at the bottom of the walkie-talkie just magnetized and pulled my chain. As the chain dropped back on my chest, it gave me a burn, leaving a v-shaped scar on my chest! Later on, we heard that the walkie-talkie had cost Ben P. or Music his life. He was gunned down like a criminal because rebels who found him with the device claimed he was on reconnaissance.

Going back to our bedroom search, when Hemson and his men looked behind our door, they saw an empty carton, thank God! I sighed inwardly. Next, we were ordered to open my two black trunks that were padlocked in the closet. I could not disclose the site of the keys because they were in my pocket book where I had also kept my official passport and some of my family pictures. My father being a Liberian envoy worked as a diplomat in a neighboring country. The dissemination of that fact would have been a sound reason for the entire family to be executed!

My mind was working like a clock. Quickly, I told this rag-tag army that I had lost the keys! So, I asked them for one of their knives to open the trunks.

Straight away, you could tell from their vicious looks! They thought they had caught us red handed, that for sure, we must be hiding weapons in those trunks! Before I could complete my request, one of them un-zippered his jacket and brought out a long sharp knife! He used it to open the trunk and started unpacking all my belongings such as unused wedding gifts, clothes, dishes etc, etc. They looked keenly with eyes like an eagle watching its prey as their guns were pointed at us! They found no weapon!

When they completed their search, on their way out through the kitchen, they saw the tiny ration of rice and canned mackerel gravy I had ditched out for our sons. One of them was about to eat the tiny piece of fish on the rice, when the commander saw him and ordered him not to touch our food or else he was going to shoot him dead! Then they all left.

At about 6 p.m., the dog started barking again! The third group appeared! It consisted of the fierce-looking Lamin and two others. This time, Lamin came with his gun on his back and a sharp butcher knife in his hand tossing it in the air. Once more, my husband ran out through the front door, I followed right behind him. Lamin was very dark in complexion. He wore a pair of long pants but without a shirt. As he opened his mouth to talk, one could see that his tongue and mouth were very red, like someone who just drank blood. We heard that this was the ritualistic practice among the rebels; they drank the blood of their enemies and consumed their organs such as the heart. They believed that this gave them strength and courage.

"Do you have any Krahn person in your house?" demanded Lamin.

"Bring him out here and I will show you what I will do to a Krahn man", he added.

We quickly responded that there was no Krahn person in our home.

At the end of all this, they asked for rice. So, I was compelled to bring the balance of the rice we had, and gave them two cups.

My husband used the opportunity to explain his function as an Assistant Professor at the University of Liberia. He even reminded them of the August 22nd incident at the University when lecturers and students were beaten up by the Doe's army.

They talked for a while and then they left.

"Lord what a day? Thank you for seeing us through. Please help us never to have an encounter like this again."

Wednesday, August 22

Today, we lost our family car, a Peugeot 504 to four heavily armed men of the Charles Taylor Rebel Group.

Four men came into our yard. "We want this car for operation" they shouted. I remembered when the first group came. Before they left, they told us to dismantle the car. My husband did, but later, we decided it wasn't worth risking our lives for. So we put all the parts back. But unknown to me, my husband had secretly removed the rotor from the car. That night, he confessed what he did. Right away, I told him to put it back very early the next day and he did.

Therefore, when the men got the car keys from us, they started the car, but it wouldn't start. So one of them opened the hood and started sucking petrol from some part of the engine. Immediately, the commander started threatening us saying that he hoped we didn't remove the rotor because if we did, he was going to kill all of us. He considered that as being tantamount to the sabotage of their operation. Fortunately, we had put the rotor back. They did some maneuvering and were able to start the car. Since they took the car, we were able to breathe some sigh of relief!

Sunday, August 26

It seemed as if Sunday in particular is a day of desecration among the rebels. Today, it has been nothing but blasting since 10a.m. The blasting has been unusually loud. We have been feeling the heavy vibrations from exploding shells and bombs all in our home. We became terrified! I was trembling and went into a state of shock! We didn't know what was going on, whether a group was advancing towards Brewerville or another retreating, we just did not know!

Later on that day, we inquired from one of our neighbors. He told us that the blasting were being carried out by the ECOWAS Force, some of whom were seen patrolling the main streets of Brewerville.

The ECOWAS Force arrived in Monrovia on August 24. They were attacked by Charles Taylor's group, so it took them one day before they could dock at the Free Port of Monrovia.

All Saturday night, we couldn't sleep we could hear all sorts of shooting and bombing. Taylor's force was attacking the ECOWAS force. "Lord, please help us to see this thing through. What is Taylor trying to do to this country and its people?"

This has been the only day so far that we have not been visited by any of the freedom fighters. On previous days, the average visit was about four or five of varied groups of fierce looking, wig-wearing, malicious, murderous, gun-toting boys and men.

The Great Escape!

Friday, August 31

At about 7:30a.m., we packed few of our belongings and decided to leave Brewerville at last! Earlier on, we had tuned to the BBC on our short wave radio. It was like the last bit of news before the batteries perished! We heard on the news that President Jerry Rawlings of neighboring Ghana was sending a ship to the Free Port of Liberia to evacuate West African nationals. We couldn't get additional details on the day and time before the batteries went totally dead! I said to myself and to the family, "that's it! We have been praying to God, this is the answer! We are leaving!"

The BBC news spread quickly like wild fire! Jockey, our neighbor's boyfriend was supposed to accompany us. At the last minute, he declined. Anyway, because we were trusting God, we didn't feel disappointed, we picked up our things and Daniel followed us carrying a five gallon-container with some water in it. We never looked back! The shrub in front of our house had grown to about two feet high. The tall rubber trees in front of our house served as some barricade and also shielded us from the red dirt road. As we got further away from our house and closer to the road, we heard the sound of a car. We peeped and saw a white pickup truck with some rag-tag soldiers in it. It was like a spontaneous reaction, we ducked immediately!

We waited until we could no longer hear the truck and began our journey to the Freeport. At about two hundred yards from our house, we came across the first check-point; it was manned by about four soldiers carrying A-K 47guns. There were two long timbers at each side of the road with some human skulls on each of the logs. At a distance, we thought we saw a long rope been tied as barricade, but as we got closer, it was actually intestines, human intestines! We were stopped instantly!

"Where your going?" one of them asked. We had to tell a lie that we were going to Logan Town, the next town over to look for food. We gave one of them $1.00, because we had nothing left, then they told us to proceed.

As we walked towards the main road, that is the Hotel Africa Road, we felt drowned in a world of silence. Each step we took was like a giant's step. We were flanked by bushes on both sides of the dirt road. The bushes were almost ten feet tall, growing lavishly by human carcasses because we could still smell them. All the houses closer to the main road were abandoned! We did not realize how left-out we were. Almost everybody else must have left Brewerville one way or the other!

After about forty minutes walk, we finally reached the junction. We had reached the coal-tarred street. We were faced with our first dilemma, which way should we go? Left or right? From where we stood, on our right, at a distance, we could see about three or four rag-tag soldiers, they looked like women. We had heard some terrible stories about their women component; they were merciless and more vicious than the men! We dared not go right.

On the left side was the open street leading to Hotel Africa, it was too open, bare and risky for us to travel on.

All of a sudden, while we stood there pondering what to do next, we saw a short stout man looking rather robust. I don't remember seeing his eyes. We asked him how to get to the Freeport. He told us not to go left or right but to cross the street and we will see a little church. Alongside the church, there's a gushing stream, we should try to cross the stream, and then walk some distance. Afterwards, we will see the old train track that will lead us to the nearest town.

Little did we know then that God must have sent an angel in disguise to guide us along the right way! I turned back to look at this stranger, he was gone! I mean he actually disappeared! He had just left us but few seconds ago!

Anyway, we followed his directions. When we got to the stream, it was a powerful gushing stream; it was flowing with tremendous force! Our little boys were almost carried away by the force of the water. They were terrified and one of them screamed. I quickly told him not to scream or we will be sought out by the bad guys.

We walked for hours on the old deserted train tracks. They looked quite narrow. On both sides of the tracks were deep trenches, that with just a slight tap on the shoulder, one could find oneself down at the bottom of the dungeons. Gradually, we started seeing people; some of them were women carrying wild vegetables on their heads to the nearest flea-market.

As we got nearer to the town of Banjo, we saw some ECOMOG soldiers wearing their white hats. We felt a little sigh of relief!

When we got to Prince Johnson's camp, one of the rival factions, we saw several stolen cars being driven up and down the road.

Unexpectedly, a brown Peugeot 505 driven by one of Prince Johnson's fairy soldiers stopped our oldest son who was walking ahead of us. The soldier was wearing a long wig and had about four or five child soldiers in the car with him. They were all wearing green camouflage uniforms.

"What's your tribe?" he asked our son.

"Bassa", he replied.

"Speak it!" commanded the wig-toting soldier.

"I can't speak it, my papa didn't teach me," replied my seven year old son.

"Go call your pa".

When we saw the scene in front of us, we became afraid. My son just stood by the car until the rest of the family got there.

"What is your tribe?" the rebel soldier asked my husband.

"Bassa", he responded.

"I hope you're not Congo-Bassa" he re-iterated.

"No", he replied and began to speak his Bassa dialect.

After some time, he told us to proceed to the check point. At the check-point, we saw several of Prince Johnson's soldiers. Many of them wore wigs and had on make-up that were stolen from homes and businesses they raided. On the side of the make-shift check-point we saw a place fenced with barb-wire where some people were being detained. Some of the unfortunate ones that they found guilty of some issues were killed right there!

We were interrogated and searched; even the water we carried in the five gallon white plastic container was looked at with suspicion. We even told the soldier to smell it, that it was only water. You could tell from the expression on his face that he was afraid.

I was praying and hoping that they shouldn't search me because I hid my passport along with some of my credentials in my under garments. Fortunately, I wasn't searched. Apart from the grace of God that was with me, my appearance looked so very emaciated, tired, aged and helpless in that with just one look at me, they let me go.

Every one of my family members was finally cleared! Off we went, back on our trail to the Freeport. We saw many people walking up and down the street and a couple of bodies littered the sides of the street.

We reached Tweh's Farm, and stopped at my relatives' place. We shared our ordeals briefly and continued on our journey.

As we got closer to the Freeport, we saw some of the undisciplined soldiers, just shooting at random. There was pandemonium, people running everywhere!

We were afraid, held the children closer and prayed not to be hit by any stray bullet!

We kept walking until we got to Mother Dukuly's Church; there we saw one of my husband's sisters, Theresa. We talked for a short while and again headed for the Port.

As we approached the Freeport, we saw tens of thousands of people thronged at the Port. I began to panic, saying, "Lord, how are we going to get out of this place to board any ship?" It looked mighty impossible!

The Free Port had two large gates, the gate on the right was barricaded with tons and tons of goods that people intended to carry out: cars, ice-boxes, equipments, television, etc, etc, whatever one can imagine. Thousands of people were facing the gate on the left. Inside the Port yard, we could see the ECOMOG soldiers and some foreign sailors. There was a smaller gate also leading into the ship yard, it remained closed. We pushed our way further into the crowd advancing toward the smaller gate. We waited for some hours in the blazing heat of the sun, not knowing what to do. As we stood there awaiting some miracle, our second son, sick and emaciated like the rest of us wanted to ease himself. My husband decided to take him away from the crowd to some patchy grassy area. I stood there with our other two sons. The 5-gallon container was between my legs with just about one and half gallons of water remaining.

All of a sudden, a lady wearing a light pink silky night-gown appeared in front of us.

"Sister, please give me some water to drink," she said.

I looked down at the water; it wasn't very much remaining for a family of five. No food, the water was all we had.

Again, I looked at the woman, but did not make eye contact. I bent down to pick the water container and immediately, the woman positioned her two hands together for me to pour the water into her hands where she would lap it. I poured the water and this lady continued drinking and wouldn't stop.

So, I said to her, "Mammy, the water not plenty o."

Then she stopped, told me "thank you yah, God bless you" and she left.

I closed the water container, set it on the ground beside me and turned around to take another look at the stranger; she was nowhere to be seen.

She couldn't have moved that far among so many people, it was just a few seconds ago she left me! Anyway, I didn't think too much of it.

All at once, like a miracle, I saw the small gate opened, and people began to queue before it. I hurriedly grabbed our two sons and joined the queue! Before we could realize what just happened, we were in the ship-yard! That stranger in the pink nightgown must have been another angel whom God must have used to bless us! My husband and our other son had not returned from using the bush.

I stood securely in the gates and began to plead with the soldier controlling the gate that my husband and son were coming.

After several minutes, I saw them pushing in to the crowd. They allowed them in along with the second group of people. Praise the Lord! We were so happy, and could smell freedom in the air!

We followed the crowd, moving towards the ship. My husband became very weak. He fell down, he could not move. I was in tears pleading that he should boost himself with whatever energy he had remaining. We cannot turn back now I said emphatically. With God's help, he got up and we started our walk slowly towards the ship.

As we got closer, I took a glimpse at the huge ship. It stood several meters in height. It was as wide as half of a football field. This was a cargo one, the kind that hauls trucks and cars. Our eyes sparkled with delight at the sight!

But getting on board, became another tug-of-war! There were two very long lines of people. On the first line, people queued up to get registered and obtain tickets. The second line consisted of ticket-bearers ready to board the ship.

It was getting to the evening hours, if we get to the tail-end of the line, it would take us almost two days to reach the front. I told my husband and sons to wait near a yellow parked car. I went to the head of the line looking at the faces of the people, trying to see if I could find any familiar faces, but none. As I almost lost hope, suddenly, I saw a Nigerian man distinguished by the tribal marks on his face, and because I could speak one of their languages, I begged him to let me stand in front of him.

"No", he said. "This spot is for my wife. But look, there is another line by the ware house, that is for women".

Truthfully, that was a shorter line. It consisted of about five women. It was hidden and one could not see it from the outside. I ran quickly and joined the line and in no time, I was standing before a naval captain cladded in white uniform and cap. He asked me for my biometrics and those of our sons and wrote the information in a big log book. Next thing I knew, he handed me a boarding ticket.

"Thank you sir," as I obtained the ticket with trembling hands.

"What about my husband?" I asked the officer.

"We are dealing only with women and children here," he responded rather harshly. In an instant, I began to cry. He had compassion on me.

"What's your husband's name?" he uttered.

"Ben," I stated nervously.

He wrote his name in the big log book and then gave me another ticket!

I was over joyous! I ran quickly to the spot where my family members were standing and broke the good news to them.

"We got tickets! We got tickets!" I exclaimed.

That was the first time in months I saw members of my family laugh! Everybody was very happy!

The next great task before us was to join the queue leading to the ship.

Looking from where we stood, there seemed to be no end to the line. It swirled around every pillar and post visible. How can we go to the end of that kind of line?

I looked at my husband and he looked at me, then as if reading my thoughts, he went to the beginning of the line, and with the last strength of a dying horse, he pushed his way in between a woman and a young man and physically got between them. As he continued to push them backwards, we all started filing in front of him. Before we knew it, we were boarding the ship for freedom!!!

Every level of the ship was filled with people seeking freedom from war. We could not see any vacant space; at last we finally landed in the hatch of the ship. It was now night time, so we spread our bed sheet that we brought along on the bare floor and the five of us were very happy to lie there without food but so happy that we had fled all the bombing and are on our way to be set free.

The next day, at about 5:30a.m., we heard the whistle of the ship: Hoop! Hoop! Hoop! Everybody started yelling and shouting and jumping for joy!

The ship set sail! We were there in the belly of the ocean for three days and three nights without food and water but very happy to be alive!

The sail for freedom wasn't without incident. On the second day, people began to panic on the ship. We heard rumors that Charles Taylor's rebels were also on board. We heard that they were going to blow the ship apart in mid-sea. We were completely helpless; the security guards on the ship were very vigilant. We saw them rounding up some men and interrogating others.

The stay on the ship was not pleasant, particularly on the second day; our place in the hatch was surrounded with human feces. People who brought food ate and ate and with no bathroom available, they just defecated all around our surroundings. We were very upset, but we kept consoling and reassuring ourselves of the freedom that was not too far away.

Emaciated, hungry, thirsty and sick, we landed on the Ghanaian soil very early in the morning of September 3, 1990. It took quite a while for the tens of thousands of people to disembark. The five of us finally got down. We prostrated and kissed the ground, thanking Almighty God to be alive.

It was like the whole act of slavery—the emancipation—men and women and children tugged and huddled in a big ship, traumatized psychologically, wounded in spirit, severely emaciated, but oh! Oh! So happy to be alive!

We were docked on another land, free of war, free of bombing, free of rag-tag army, so free, free, and free at last!!!!!

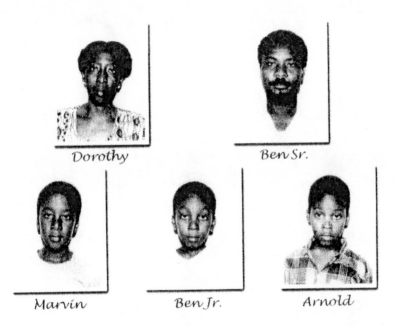

Dorothy   Ben Sr.

Marvin   Ben Jr.   Arnold

The First set of pictures taken when we landed
in Ghana September 3, 1990.

Conclusion

The 21st century has met many countries both in the Developed and Developing countries competing for advancement in space program and computer technology. This is not the case with Liberia. Regrettably, the loss of precious lives and the levels of destruction in the Liberian Civil War had thrown the country some centuries back into the Dark Age.

Like a broken record, the thoughts keep playing in my mind over and over again. I think about the consequences. How hundreds of thousands of innocent people have died in the hands of men and women armed with guns, swords and knives. Many Liberians have become refugees in neighboring countries and in the United States. I think about innocent mothers and their babies who sought shelter at the Lutheran Church, but were gunned down with their babies still clenched to their backs.

I think about the child soldiers, young boys hardly in their teens, given guns and dosed with drugs, who became killers even of their own family members. How can these children be rehabilitated? They saw and carried out too many atrocities in their short lives.

Elaborating from another perspective, Stewart, 1992 pointed out that the saddest result of the Liberian Civil War has been its effect on the children. Accordingly, she said many have been killed, thousands died of starvation or disease and many young children have suffered permanent brain damage because of the lack of good food. They also suffered psychological damage as thousands of them witnessed the rapes of their mothers, aunts and sisters. They have been terrorized as they watched their fathers and brothers taken outside their homes and shot. The scars left by these memories will never vanish.

I think about hundreds of young girls and women who became victims of rape, gave birth to children they didn't plan for and how many of them were ravished by sexually transmitted diseases such as HIV AIDS.

I also think about women who were forcibly taken from their families by rebels who turned them into cooks and sex-partners.

I think about thousands of children who have been orphaned, their parents signaled out and killed for the mere criterion of being either an Americo-Liberian or a Gio or even emanating from the Krahn tribe.

My heart goes out to hundreds of thousands of Liberians who suffer silently from posttraumatic stress disorder, who without treatment may not be able to recover successfully and live fuller and happier lives.

Liberians were generally known as very friendly, peace-loving people who love to have a good time. How have these traits and characteristics suddenly changed to deep hearted hatred, so bitter and cruel that men disemboweled pregnant women who were fellow citizens and smashed their un-born babies to death! It seemed so unbelievable!

I believe no single person or group can be totally blamed. The rage had been built for several years due to segregation, lack of wide-spread education of the majority of the populace, economic deprivation, poverty, corruption, nepotism etc.

Lessons should be learned from the Liberian Civil War, and the Rwandan genocide. According to Dallaire (2003), the toxic ethnic extremism that infected Rwanda was a deep-rooted and formidable foe, built from colonial discrimination and exclusion, envy, racism etc.

He said that although no single person or group is blamed for the causes of the war, nonetheless, those who planned and executed the war should not be exonerated or go scotch free.

Dallaire also pointed to the fact that the youth of the Third World will no longer tolerate living in circumstances that give them no hope for the future.

The waste of war may never be replenished especially in the developing countries. Valuable lives of loved ones can never be brought back to life.

The resources such as money and diamonds used in buying ammunition, guns, bombs and other war equipment could have been used to develop the country, create more jobs and in essence, improve the lives of the people.

The healing process would begin when Liberians can find a spot in their hearts to forgive each other, embrace each other and work hard together for a better future for our youths and those yet to be born.

Quite recently, U.S. educated economist and former finance minister Ellen Johnson-Sirleaf won the second round of Liberian presidential election in November 2005. In January 2006, she was inaugurated as Africa's first elected woman head of state. I have often asked. Can she intensify the healing by uniting Liberians and eradicate the two divisions?

In the past, Liberian leaders were men who have betrayed the trust and confidence imposed in them. Most of them have used the people as pawns, shed innocent blood, and exploited hard working citizens for their personal aggrandizement. Can our first female president cause a change for the better?

Ellen Johnson-Sirleaf has declared "zero tolerance" of corruption. Can we now be hopeful that the country's resources would be judiciously used and development programs distributed throughout the country?

Finally, war is never a resolution to conflict. I feel a sense of loss in the Liberian Civil War especially for my generation who has lost their rightful places in the Liberian Society. I also feel a sense of loss for our children who have lost their culture, friendship peers and the sense of pride for their country. Losses suffered by victims of war can never be replenished. Maybe the visible scars can be healed. Can the invisible ones be healed too? Sometimes I wonder.

Ellen Johnson–Sirleaf—the first elected black female president in Africa and current president of Liberia.

Terms/Acronyms

A.F.L.—Armed Forces of Liberia

B.T.C.—Barclay Training Center

ECOMOG—Military wing of ECOWAS developed to enforce peace keeping in the region.

ECOWAS—Economic Commission of West African States

NPFL—National Patriotic Front of Liberia, the major rebel group in the Liberian Civil War. It was headed by Charles Taylor.

Palava Hut—Hut with thatched roof set aside in the village for purpose of recreation and the settlement of disputes.

SATU—Special Anti Terrorist Unit–the specialized group of soldiers trained in Israel to protect Samuel Doe.

References

Bodnarchuk, Kari, 2000. Rwanda, Country Torn Apart. Minneapolis, MN. Lerner Publications Company.

Chieh-Johnson, Dorothy, 1987. A Study of Rural Fertility Among Some Ethnic Groups In Liberia with Special Emphasis on the Intermediate Variables.

Chieh-Johnson, Dorothy and Cross, Anne, et al. 1988. Liberian Demographic and Health Survey 1986. Ministry of Planning and Economic Affairs/Institute for Resource Development, Columbia, Maryland, U.S.A.

Dallaire, Romeo, 2005. Shake Hands with the Devil. New York, NY. Carroll and Graf Publishers.

Ilibagiza, Immaculee, 2006. Left to Tell. Carlsbad, California. Hay House, Inc.

Levy, Patricia, 1998. Cultures of the World Liberia. New York. Marshall Gavendish Corporation.

Liberia Country Study. Fred P.M. Van der Kraaij, 1983. "The Open Door Policy of Liberia. An Economic history of modern Liberia." 18 July 2007. <http://www.globalsecurity.org/military/library/1985>

Map of Liberia, 1997-2006. 14 August 2007. <http://www.canadiancontent.net/profiles/liberia.html>

Rozario, Paul, 2003. Countries of the World, Liberia. Milwaukee, Wisconsin. Gareth Stevens Publishing.

Stewart, Gail B., 1992. Liberia. New York. Crestwood House.

Photo Credits

Samuel K. Doe and some of his gallant men/Joseph Tellewoyan: 53;
http://en.wikipedia.org/

Ellen Johnson-Sirleaf/ 57;
http://missliberiacalifornia.org/images/the_president_a3h6.png

Cover design- Eric Moore, May, 2007. Methuen, Massachusetts.

978-0-595-47288-8
0-595-47288-5

Printed in the United States
97948LV00004B/82-84/A